SYNAPTIC

Ᏼ∩ᏏᎠ

OSKANA POETRY *&* POETICS

Alison Calder

# *Synaptic*

University of Regina Press

Cover art: "mondo, hi tech, sfondo, internet, comunicazione" by XYZ+ / Adobe Stock

Cover and text design: Duncan Campbell, University of Regina Press

Editor: Randy Lundy
Proofreader: Donna Grant

The text and titling faces are Arno, designed by Robert Slimbach.

Library and Archives Canada Cataloguing in Publication

Title: Synaptic / Alison Calder.

Names: Calder, Alison, 1969- author.

Series: Oskana poetry & poetics ; 14.

Description: Series statement: Oskana poetry & poetics ; 14

Identifiers: Canadiana (print) 2021039062X | Canadiana (ebook) 20210390646 | ISBN 9780889778610 (softcover) | ISBN 9780889778627 (PDF) | ISBN 9780889778634 (EPUB)

Subjects: LCGFT: Poetry.

Classification: LCC PS8605.A455 S96 2022 | DDC C811/.6—dc23

Canada Council   Conseil des arts
for the Arts      du Canada

Canadä

creative
SASKATCHEWAN

UNIVERSITY OF REGINA PRESS
University of Regina
Regina, Saskatchewan
Canada S4S 0A2
TELEPHONE: (306) 585-4758
FAX: (306) 585-4699
WEB: www.uofrpress.ca
EMAIL: uofrpress@uregina.ca

We acknowledge the support of the Canada Council for the Arts for our publishing program. We acknowledge the financial support of the Government of Canada. / Nous reconnaissons l'appui financier du gouvernement du Canada. This publication was made possible with support from Creative Saskatchewan's Book Publishing Production Grant Program.

*for Warren, as always*

# CONTENTS

## Connectomics

3    Connectomics

4    CLARITY

5    *C. elegans*

7    Silent Synapse

8    Infinity

9    Science

10    Functional Specialization

11    Glia

12    Hebb's Postulate: A Love Poem

13    Semantic Selectivity

14    Natural Narrative

15    Engram

16    Trials

17    Wellbutrin

18    Synaptic Cleft

19    Flattened Cortex

20    Pycortex

21    Optogenetics

22    Neuroinformatics

23    File Drawer Problem

24    Chimera

25    Chimera 2

26    Area X

27    Lectotype

28    Supercharged

29    Somatoparaphrenia

30    High Vocal Centre

31    Cryptic Maladaptation

32    32 Public Fears

33    "The Greater Mystery"

34 *Chlamydomonas reinhardtii*
35 The Anna Karenina Principle/The Fragility of Good Things
36 The Modified Anna Karenina Principle

**Other Fires**

39 Argument with Agnes Martin *(Siberia/Saskatchewan)*
40 Argument with Agnes Martin *(Taos)*
41 Three Marriages: I and the Village
44 The Storm
45 Foundling
46 Foundling 2
47 Selkie
48 Troll
49 Rumours of Bears
50 At 50
51 In the '70s
52 The Future
53 Lobster
54 University Bulletin
55 Melt
56 Warming
57 Crawling
58 Comets
59 Winter, and the River
60 Opening
61 Throwaway
62 Non-villanelle for the Tide
63 Causeway
64 Mass Ascension
65 The Shape
66 At El Santuario de Chimayó

71 *Notes to the Poems*
73 *Acknowledgements*

*Connectomics*

CONNECTOMICS[1]


The idea is
to render the brain
transparent enough to read through,
trickles of water washing away thought.

Deletions, insertions, translocations, inversions,
proofreaders' symbols carve a straight line
to the minotaur.

In the light of the laboratory,
thought's skein unravels,
bumpy road smoothed.

Lucent, pellucid, the brain wavers
like the glass in a display case,
minimum interference between eye and page.

Like reading through a jellyfish.
The text, however, remains opaque.

---

1  Roughly speaking, the goal of connectomics is to improve
ways to map the neural connections in the brain.

Firefly mouse flickers, forgets
lessons, forgets
want. Inside his skull
the past incinerates, embers
blizzarding into ash.
The screened brain's a maze,
sizzling, fragments
of a film that's not replayed.
*What* and *how* and *why* flash briefly,
die. Mouse mind flares.
It turns to glass.

2    CLARITY is the name of the process by which the brain
is made transparent. Splicing firefly genes into mice makes
neural mapping easier because parts of the brain will fluoresce.
These mice are particularly used for Alzheimer's research.

## C. ELEGANS[3]

You call us simple.
On TV, innocents scream at cartoon germs,
brandish cleansers, scrub us away.
Grade six science classes learn what's living
in their lashes, are traumatized for life.
Still, I have what you need.
Complicated, tractable, I am the ideal
compromise between *like* and *not*.
I'm useful because I die quickly:
your funding agencies approve.
Plumbing for secrets in my glassy body,
you peer through my window
seeking 40 percent of your soul.
*How age? How sleep? How want?*
—the fundamental mysteries of biology
hidden in plain sight.

The manual says *keep your samples separate from your culture.*
But let me reverse your gaze, turn
the microscope upon the viewer.
My elegant curves, the symmetries
of my crystalline motility, mesmerize.
Rotund, rotating, I root into regions
you've not been to. My eyeless face
recognizes light.

---

3   *Caenorhabditis elegans,* a small soil-dwelling nematode, was the first
animal to have its genome completely sequenced. Forty percent
of its genome is identical to that of humans. All 959 somatic
cells of its transparent body are visible under a microscope.

Hermaphrodite, I love myself.
Non-hazardous, non-infectious, non-pathogenic,
        non-parasitic,
of no economic importance, I'm nothing
that you are.

Ghost owl, death owl, recognizable
by its mask, the silent flight
that is like ours.

Evil omen, devil owl,
spirit with a heart-shaped face,
whose eyes shine blackly
over night fields.

Straw owl, rat owl, whose rasp
doesn't ask a question.
It knows itself
and you.

Stone owl, whose stare erases.
It sees you and doesn't care.

---

4    Aside from the human brain, some of the model systems
used for connectomics research are the mouse, the fruit
fly, the nematode *C. elegans*, and the barn owl. A silent
synapse is one that will not connect in a measurable way.

After we exhausted wonder
we shut down the computers, turned off the lights.
Everything was known.
The lab gleamed.
No dust or grit, no sand left in the bucket
to remind us of the beach.
No wet towels thrown on the floor
because we had to get somewhere right away.
The shiny fingerprints I left on the phone
because I couldn't wait to tell you
what would happen next
were gone. We let the air out
of the balloons left over from the surprise party
because there was no more surprise.
We revised the dictionary, removed *curiosity*,
replaced *speculation* with *retrospection*.
We grew our knowledge right up to the end.
When we got to the limit, we stopped.

---

5   "Someday a fleet of microscopes will capture every neuron
and every synapse in a vast database of images, and someday
artificially intelligent supercomputers will analyze the
images without human assistance, to summarize them in a
connectome. I do not know, but I hope that I will live to see that
day." —Sebastian Seung, TED Talk "I Am My Connectome."

# SCIENCE[6]

A road, a network, consciousness
is a computer, a map.
It's a vehicle on a road, it's not the road.
It's a stream.
A neuron's like a tree. Consciousness
is a load the vehicle's hauling.
It's water (it's not water). It's a turtle
in a shell, and also it's the shell.
It's a cable, a cord tying things down in a truck box
so they don't fly out.
The brain is like spaghetti, a giant 3D colouring book.
You're a kite and it's the wind. Maybe it's the string.
A synapse is two friends talking on the phone.
The brain's an eavesdropper.
The skull's a box of books you move
from house to house to house.

---

6   "Let's return from the heights of metaphor, and return to
    science." —Sebastian Seung, TED Talk "I Am My Connectome."

# FUNCTIONAL SPECIALIZATION[7]

The brain is not, as you might think,
a bag of goo.
It is a dense constellation
of carefully mapped drawers.
Here is your speech. Here, your fine motor skills.
Here, the summer you're eleven
and you and your father sit on the dock
watching sheet lightning define the lake's horizon
for what might be hours. It's a hot night;
rough boards scratch your sunburned legs
and catch the seat of your bathing suit.
Later, the storm will turn on you, hailstones
big as eggs breaking the windows
in the back of the cabin, the grass a mess of glass and ice.
But now the storm is far enough away that
there's no thunder, your father's words settling alongside
faint, steady ripples. What he's saying's
not important. The whole sky's a theatre
you watch together.
You've never seen anything like it.

---

7   Functional specialization suggests that particular
areas in the brain control different functions.

GLIA[8]

After Grandma died, I stripped the sheets from the spare bed
and beneath them found more sheets.
The linen cupboard's layers burst
with threadbare towels, faint traces of old scent.
The sewing room downstairs was packed with scraps,
acrylic yarn left over from the bonnet
in my fat-faced toddler photo, the button jar
an archaeology of fashion.
It was impossible to pack: no suitcase
had a handle or a working latch.
Grandma's thrifty soul exposed, I analyzed,
I diagnosed, drank endless cups of tea
from endless teacups, until
exhausted, heartless, someone called the auctioneer.

Cleaning out her closet, I found a jagged paint line on the wall
where steps used to be. Stairway
to nowhere, plaster and lath below old wallpaper.
My mind tried to rearrange the furniture.
A house could move, not solid but elastic.
The closet was a door, the Earth was round,
not flat. As layered as the spare-room bed,
the button jar, the other scraps
I'd looked at and discarded.

8    "Glia ... are the cells that provide support to the neurons. In much
     the same way that the foundation, framework, walls, and roof of
     a house provide the structure through which run various electric,
     cable, and telephone lines, ... not only do glia provide the structural
     framework that allows networks of neurons to remain connected,
     they also attend to the brain's various housekeeping functions
     (such as removing debris after neuronal death)." —R. Stufflebeam,
     "Neurons, Synapses, Action Potentials, and Neurotransmission"

# HEBB'S POSTULATE: A LOVE POEM[9]

Cells that fire together,
wire together.

---

9    Hebb's postulate states that when cells act in concert, the
     bonds between them are strengthened. Conversely, cells that
     act at different times show no increased bond strength.

parents murdered
children convicted

wife killed
husband confessed

children murdered
wife confessed

husband killed
parents convicted

parents killed
children confessed

wife murdered
husband convicted

children killed
husband confessed

husband murdered
parents confessed

---

10   Brain imaging may allow scientists to chart which parts of the
     cerebral cortex are active in response to the meaning of particular
     words. This localized reaction is called semantic selectivity. "For
     example, on the left-hand side of the brain, above the ear, is one of
     the tiny regions that represents the word 'victim.' The same region
     responds to 'killed,' 'convicted,' 'murdered' and 'confessed.' On the
     brain's right-hand side, near the top of the head, is one of the brain
     spots activated by family terms: 'wife,' 'husband,' 'children,' 'parents.'"

Girl in a red hood, with wolf and forest.
Children, orphaned, in the oven.
One beautiful woman trying to kill another.
Truths, they say, the core disguised
as faery. Story growing innocently from itself
like a wick dipped in wax.
Say it again.
The young are cursed by their elders,
animals drive hard bargains.
Story takes on life as flesh fruits around a pit,
tumorous, rotting.
Say how this girl pricks her finger, this one
wants to dance. Her feet cut off.
Strangler story like a vine, glorious,
gangrenous, deliberately unfurling
a glass coffin to show off beauty.
Steal her skin and she'll be yours, say how
when she walks it feels like knives.
Beneath this story is another, and another
under that: nature's ground is shaky,
emperor's clothes threatening to slip.
Say how these truths are like an apple,
with poison at its hollow core.

11    In order to map semantic selectivity, subjects were monitored
        while they listened to stories described as "natural narratives" for
        two hours. A "natural" narrative contains a story's "basic narrative
        elements such [as] plot, setting, characterization and speech...
        [and] has not been manipulated in any premeditated way."

ENGRAM[12]

Memory shimmers, translucent,
just out of reach. The weary traveller,
seeing light in the marsh, yearns for home,
warmth, his mother, bread that steams
when she breaks it, a bowl of milk
waiting beside the white plate, his feet
in their school shoes swinging carefully,
cat purring under his chair, soup heating
on the stove, which is always ready
to dry his mittens, hanging handless
and wet from new snow

                    even as he thinks that
he's lost, clothes binding, feet sinking,
mud, rocks, reeds reeling him
into breathless embrace.
Will-o'-the-wisp, fool's fire,
you do damage, carrying that torch
to the edge of the precipice,
you kindle the past we think we live in.
Insubstantial, synecdochic,
we're looking for ourselves.
Of course we'll follow you.

---

12   An engram is the mechanism that stores memory traces
     as biophysical or biochemical changes in the brain. It
     is not known exactly where in the brain engrams can
     be found, and some scientists speculate that the entire
     brain may be an engram. Engram structure is sometimes
     explained as being analogous to that of a hologram, in that
     any part of a hologram contains the whole hologram.

Fear of home, fear of kitchens,
fear of perfume, fear of spice.
Fear of sun, of light.
Fear of cleaners and soap.
Fear of spring. Fear of green and yellow.
Fear of knives and glasses,
shaving, showers.
Fear of candies, fear of toothpaste,
fear of darkness, fear of dreams.

13   Mapping fear memories can reveal engram location. To
create fear memories under controlled conditions, scientists
subject patients to electric shocks while introducing unique
scents like lemon or mint. Later, scientists monitor the
patients' reactions to these scents as the patients sleep.

Say hello to my little friends,
the blue and white buddies
with whom I take my daily walk.
Pea-sized superheroes, non-caped crusaders,
they save my day, measure my week
in plastic clicks. They put the lid
on the jack-in-the-box, muzzle
the dogs. They keep my umbrella
right side in. Rain or shine,
they've got me.

---

14    Wellbutrin is a brand name for the antidepressant bupropion.

Awash in neuron surge, chemistry's riptide,
slammed on the sand, yanked back
and thrown, again and again:
it's not easy floating.
Water's a bridge
you can't walk on.
Hung up, flung out: no way
to hurry a slow gate's opening,
hasten the flow. All dams
eventually fail, but an impulse
can't be communicated without resistance.
So dig that hole.
Now: a message in a bottle, and you
without a lifejacket,
current pulling you one way,
down.

---

15   A synaptic cleft is the small gap between two neurons, across
which information passes. Signals from one neuron flow into
the gap, and when the gap is flooded, the signal drains into
the next neuron. The signal can only flow one direction.

A grand piano dropped from a window,
the echoing gong of hammers on strings,
all the symphonies all at once:
the ironed brain uncreases.
Thought, released, collides,
the palette of the colour wheel
collapsing into mud.
Metaphors unstack: the poem
is an ocean inside out. How now
describe the nesting doll,
the one inside that looks like you?

16 Because the human cortex is so highly folded and layered, it
is difficult to read data when it is presented in a 3D model.
One way to render this data more readable is to use a
computer model to flatten the cortex into two dimensions.
Scientific data can then be mapped onto this flat brain.

The spare room's quilt is built from scraps,
translucent. Cotton, corduroy,
these are the textures of 1998,
when Dad no longer filled his shirts
and they hung empty in the closet.
Nothing matches. Patches
of stripes, dots, tiny brown triangles
and squares faded to abstraction,
paler versions of themselves
trailing off into nothing.
To make a quilt you layer:
first piece the top, then add the fill and backing.
The quilting is the stitch.
Beneath the squares, the seams are full
of hidden fabric. If you ripped apart
the sutures, laid the fragments side by side,
you could assemble the resemblance
of a blanket, see where it might hold a body.
Pulled back to rags, it won't keep anybody warm.

---

17   Pycortex is an open source software used to translate
     information about the brain, specifically that from
     fMRI and other volumetric data, into a model that
     is easier to visualize than a traditional 3D map.

# OPTOGENETICS[18]

Let there be light!
Non-surgical strike, unmanned drone
spiking my skull's desert.
Shot of oil to quiet
the brain's hamster wheel,
settle the pop pop pop
of my bursting thoughts.
Autonomy's not all it's cracked up
to be, surrender now to someone else
flipping the switch, follow
that flashlight's laser beam.
Tag! I'm it, chasing
the flash, bam!

From beneath, phosphorescent fish
become invisible, their glow melting
into the ocean's plastic underside.
That's what I want, a boneless slide
into camouflage, only reflections
looking in.

---

18   Optogenetics uses a burst of light to affect genetically
     sensitized neurons in the brain, so that researchers can
     manipulate a subject's moods or behaviours.

The brain's a bin,
a barn, basin
and drain. It's host
and hostage, brim
and lid. Not hammer
nor nail, baby nor pram.
It's net and nib, railing
and stair. Not pail nor rain,
but jailer and jail.

19 Studying the brain generates so much data that regular
recording systems can't keep up. Neuroinformatics
marries neuroscience and computer science to produce
new ways of organizing and understanding the patterns
in this dense, quickly moving information.

Think outside the box, but then
you'd better crawl back in.
Blue sky thinking only leads to clouds.
A man's reach should exceed his grasp—
Just kidding. No one likes a loser.
Let's optimize and synchronize, out-of-step Rockettes
kicked to the curb. Our metrics
don't measure failure, so step on solid ground.
Climbing without a rope won't get you anywhere.
Stay in harness.
Holes in the floor? Keep walking,
eyes on the prize, tri-council Cerberus
barking at the door.

20 The term "file drawer problem" is shorthand for positive-
results bias, a type of publication bias that skews
researchers into reporting only research that has positive
results. Authors are more likely to submit, editors more
likely to accept, and granting agencies more likely to fund
reports of positive outcomes than those with negative
or inconclusive results. The main sources of research
funding in Canada are the Social Sciences and Humanities
Research Council, the Natural Sciences and Engineering
Research Council, and the Medical Research Council.

Autocleave heats,
mousetakes cartograft.
Mark this: in *neuvo*science, it's genedict,
identifraction packed in a spiral suitcase.
*Nouveau*-logist, embryoidering,
noodling with needles, nuclear
witch graft. New pattern
humonetized:
A N D.

---

21   A genetic chimera has genetic material that results from
combining elements from the DNA of two or more separate
zygotes. A chimera may be produced through genetic
manipulation or organ transplantation, among other means.
Chimeric mice are an important tool for biological research.

When one-eyed Polyphemus asks Odysseus his name,
he answers *no man,*
the original "who's on first?"

Trapped in the cave, Odysseus
speaks monstrously. He is not himself.

To get out of the hole,
he grabs an animal, hangs on.
Polyphemus, groping at the cave's mouth,
feels only beast:
*No man has blinded me.*

---

22   In classical Greek mythology, a chimera is a monster made
up of a goat, a lion, and a serpent. The word "chimera" also
means something that is impossible and cannot exist.

Illiterate's signature,
perpetual stand-in, landing pad
for everything.
The dead-eyed stare, the treasure.
Busy intersection of practice
and performance, twixt
kiss and corpse, starter's pistol
and finish line. The map.
Let X equal.

---

23   Humans and songbirds share the ability to learn
through cultural transmission; songbirds learn songs
as humans learn language. One of the areas in the brain
where this ability is located in songbirds is a particular
part of the basal ganglia known as "Area X."

# LECTOTYPE[24]

The goal is actually
to render the brain
opaque, a solid block
of wood to knock on.

If we can see there's something
in the nothing, the astronaut
is tethered, space filled
beside the synapse.

Adam's language, immovable.
Each name must have a string to follow.
Pin the tail on the donkey, anchor
the word in the thing.

The real is a series of vanishing points.
In the specimen drawer, a drawing.
A magician opens his hands:
the bird is gone.

---

24    Mapping the brain is like naming all the animals. The rules of
naming are governed by the International Commission on
Zoological Nomenclature, which seeks to universalize and
clarify the labelling of all animals. A lectotype is a zoological
specimen that serves as the single type specimen for a species.
For example, one individual meadowlark preserved somewhere
in the world serves as a lectotype, so that the question "what is
*Sturnella neglecta*?" can be answered by presenting that specimen.
However, in cases where an actual specimen is not available,
as with the Réunion parakeet, extinct since 1770, a written
description or historical illustration may serve as a lectotype.

Where the rubber hits the road, the need
for speed is the dream of flight.
Smoking stink and punishment of noise
is the blind desire to get out, get up,
away from bodies, our own, the others,
those whining and grasping, their mouths.
The terror of the land-locked, the drive
to get through the closing door, shave off
the flesh. If we were pure. If we were numbers,
repeatable. The need for speed
is a swaddling of the self, senses overrun.
Ladle it on, cacophony, assault the eyes,
the ears. The heart of noise is silence.
Deafened, speechless, pedal to the metal,
we claw our way to the cyclone's interior,
pulsing cocoon trying to bust out some wings.

-----

25   "Richard Mooney's grandfather, a mechanical engineer,
     couldn't imagine why birds would be useful for understanding
     the human brain. 'The same way that taking apart a one-
     cylinder lawn mower can prepare you for how a supercharged
     v8 in a Formula One racer works,' explained Mooney, a
     neurobiologist at Duke University Medical Center."

If I believe that the hand is mine, then
I must be prepared to use it.
Numbness, daily insulation against others,
forced touching in a packed subway car.
From the other end, shouts: a woman
haranguing a drunk, everyone looking
elsewhere. I consider my arm: it connects me
to this car, as we hang off-balance, swaying
synchronously, or suddenly clattering together
like bowling pins struck by a fast-moving ball.
Reposition, reblanking our eyes.
On the seat backs, grease, fingerprints, other people's hair.
Grotesqueries of other lives.
A man lies on the floor of the car, shoes, no socks,
sleeping something off.
My arm connects me to the same bar
everyone holds, strap around my wrist
keeping me standing. If I acknowledge that
I can hook, or grab, or hold,
then I have to acknowledge I am choosing
one of these things, the fist, the open palm.
A stranger strokes someone's hand, I can't tell if it's mine.

---

26 Somatoparaphrenia is a condition in which patients deny
ownership of parts of their bodies. Researchers at the
Universities of Milan and Turin analyzed the rubber hand
illusion, in which they stroked a rubber hand that was visible
to a subject at the same time as they also stroked the subject's
own hidden hand. The brain's ability to control the real hand
was diminished as it identified itself with the false one.

All actions are sequential, tick-tock
of a burning clock. Mind metronomes
the heartbeat, gaps between the puncta.
Like dominoes, bird notes tip,
music spilling like Pandora's box, each tone
a second closer to the end.
Cause and effect unscrolls like a player piano.

Let's freeze the tempo,
slow down the scale,
aim time's arrow back at the quiver.
Release the day,
the week, the month.
Refurl those fronds, set sun
before it rises, the crow
the rooster swallows.

27  Because of its prolific breeding capability, the zebra
    finch is widely studied and, in 2008, became the second
    bird after the chicken to have its genome sequenced.
    Among other things, researchers study it to discover
    how the brain's timing mechanism works, by cooling
    portions of the bird's brain to slow down its song. The
    portion cooled is called the high vocal centre.

Tea, not coffee.
Gin, not rum.
Still, not sparkling.
In high school, typing
instead of German: was it that?
Reading, thinking, impossible
to parse the sentence, looping cause and effect.
Was it turning left, not right,
standing up, not sitting down, that caused
that butterfly to flap its wings?
Coke or Pepsi. Fries or salad. Somewhere,
a tipping point, snowpack shifting,
far-off growl that I don't yet hear.

---

28  Cryptic maladaptation is a hidden genetic vulnerability
    only exposed by unknown and extreme future events.

Alien abduction, board games, body (finding one),
clowns, directions (faulty), emotions (visible),

feral dogs, flash floods, grocery avalanche,
hair (in mouth), identity (stolen), jokes (unfunny), killers (serial),

locker room, missed meeting, no pants,
other people, pull doors (pushing), questions (awkward),

rules (broken), singalong, spontaneous combustion,
tripe (accidentally ordering), unseen stair, unusual smells, violins,

wetness (other people's), wetness (own), wrong team (cheering for),
x-ray vision, youth (clinging to), zealots.

---

29   Some studies discerned a predictable order within divergent
     maladaptations. One study of stress factors examined 19 public
     fears, such as terrorism and rising crime, to determine that, in
     a time of crisis, these fears were both intensified and spread
     more widely, as different people began to fear the same thing.

Too early to hear pebbles
dropped in the well
or to draw up the sounding line.

Too early to count dogs
barking at 10 pm or lights
coming on over Broadway.

Too early for the chemistry in the cookie,
the hive inside the bees.

Chickens in the eggs, birds
in the hand: not yet. Not time
for haystacks in the needle
and forests in the trees.

Set the alarm and call me when it rings.
I'm going to sleep for a long time.

---

30   In 2015, John Colapinto interviewed Karl Deisseroth, a leading
     figure in optogenetics, for *The New Yorker*. "Deisseroth told
     me that he is no closer to understanding the greater mystery
     of the mind: how a poem or a piece of music can elicit
     emotions from a mass of neurons and circuits suspended
     in fats and water. 'Those are all incredibly important
     questions,' he said. 'It's just too early to ask them.'"

Who knew so much of nature
is electric?
Eels, fireflies, the tip
of the iceberg.
Apparently the world is made of light,
that's not a metaphor.
It's a hot mirror getting hotter.
Still, glowing mice don't get too far
outside the lab, spotlit snack
on a midnight flit.
They're not the problem,
the background makes them vulnerable.
We'd never see them
if we flipped a switch, lit up
every living thing.

---

31   *Chlamydomonas reinhardtii*, a single-celled alga, can
     thrive in total darkness but also has an "eyespot" that
     senses light. Its entire nuclear genome sequence was
     published in 2007. It is a model organism for studying
     how cells respond to light and was instrumental in the
     discovery of channelrhodopsin2 (ChR2), an algal protein
     that was central to the development of optogenetics.

## THE ANNA KARENINA PRINCIPLE/
## THE FRAGILITY OF GOOD THINGS[32]

Finally, proof of what you always suspected:
there *are* more rainy days than sunny ones,
the grass *was* greener somewhere else.
Your brother got the bigger piece.
You won't be promoted, or married
for long. Divorce is in the stacked cards.
Cakes are mostly burnt, broths are mostly spoiled,
the fish don't bite more often than they do.
Your bus is the last to come. Other lines move faster.
Other people's dogs bark less, other cats purr more.
You drop more stitches than you knit.
Still, you're bound to win
if you bet against yourself.

32  The Anna Karenina principle gets its name from Tolstoy's
    novel, which opens with the line, "Happy families are all alike;
    every unhappy family is unhappy in its own way." The principle
    indicates that while successful adaptations within a group
    are all alike, maladaptations can happen in myriad ways. In
    catastrophe theory, this appears as the principle of the fragility
    of all good things, where good things, which require a number
    of elements to be coordinated in order to exist, are more fragile
    than bad things, which have the power to cause chaos.

Salt is pepper, hawks are handsaws,
the living are the dead.
We act like money, everyone holding hands
in the middle of the Venn diagram.
Nothing metaphysical now
about the yoking of dissimilars,
rough edges all ground into a smoothie.
We move as a herd, a happy family.
The grass is the same green everywhere,
animals ubiquitous, birds flocking together.
Everyone's hemlines rise and fall,
bulls lying down with the bears.
Forget the trees. Look at the forest.
This murmuration, everyone
asking for directions at the same time.

---

33   The modified Anna Karenina principle suggests that although
     maladaptations are all different, they follow the same structures.
     To investigate this similarity, scientists brought together
     studies of groups of humans, animals, trees, grassy plants,
     stock market prices, and changes in the banking sector.

*Other Fires*

# ARGUMENT WITH AGNES MARTIN

*(Siberia/Saskatchewan)*


Driving home across the prairies in January,
white shimmers above pale grasses,
tints blue, then cream, then washes out.
White sky, white ground furrowed.
Slough weeds are café-au-lait, intricate
henna designs, thin lines gridding over the snow
in a series of triangles. The slide from blue to brown.
Nothing is pure white, no purity but shape.
Telephone poles repeat, train tracks, highway edge
confirms the horizon. *Lines, grids, and fields*
*of extremely subtle color* seen through fence wire,
the greys of a falling-down barn.
Similarity, difference, the same shapes punched out over and over.
Scrape away white: pink, green, cream, thin blue
of powdered milk. The minimal aesthetic. Plain.

# ARGUMENT WITH AGNES MARTIN

*(Taos)*

Desert to desert, dust to dust,
everywhere ruins, you can get tetanus
just looking at pictures of this place.
Rusted metal, rusted earth, wood dessicating
into weightlessness. Colours bleached,
collapsing barn sage grey. No accident the sky,
the blaring light, the monstrous quality of scale.
Haphazard structures face different directions, uncaring.
You step into the smell of spice,
grasshoppers splash against you, you hear
the *chrk-chrk* of magpies squabbling in the weeds.
Drought scours your sight, your skin, oasis visible
60 miles away. You won't go there.
What you're facing is where you're from.

I.

The man and horse love each other,
you can't say differently,
four-fingered groom with a flower fist, horse
absent-mindedly opening its mouth
to eat the bouquet.

A woman, topsy-turvy, goes off
with the man holding the sickle: he must be death,
the corpse-green groom in another disguise.
She protests in vain.

Below them, a half-full moon waits
to be tipped over houses strung like bunting along the hill.
Is it a party, that wistful man in his orange pyjamas
caught by his halo in the church door?
The white-lipped groom is reaching,
ring shining red on his truncated hand.
His gift is an ice cream he'll lick till it's gone.

II.

The woman floats, a balloon no one wants.
Death is marching her out of the scene.

III.

But what do you make of that other woman,
milking the goat by the horse's cheek?
Half-turned, she lifts her pail. Is her hand, in its mitten,
hiding the groom's red ring? Her striped skirt
is solid above the electric bouquet.
Is she the third bride?
She might be the horse's dream,
that comforting forehead against the side,
drawing warm milk in a shadowed stable
below the clock face in the horse's eye.

The bride aghast, the women aghast,
white ribbons whipping in the wind,
no husband but a hole in the ground.
In the happy house light spills like tears from the windows.
This is the moment when the ship sinks,
train derails, time's blade cleaves.
The women, frozen, hands on their faces,
bride's forgotten dress flapping in the mud.
Her ribbons, soiled, are spoiled,
petals peeling from a flower crown.
There is no help.
If they could unspin the silk, reweave
the cocoon, respool the thread inside the worm,
they could return the ship to shore, call back
the train to station. Go back to *before*.
When they move, it will be *after*.

Another story. Night, a ship
driven onto rock.
Among the breaking timbers,
heaving surge of water's giant fist,
a strobing flash of lightning shows
one thing that can be saved, small
package passed from desperate hand
to hand: a baby.

Nothing else.

Anonymous parcel with no return address,
landless, nameless, face recalling
features of the dead.
Unmoored. That baby could be anything,
from bastard prince to king. Foundling,
jettisoned into a future.
Who will take him in?
Shepherd boy or merchant, he'll sleep
with animals or else on feather beds,
he'll be written on or write.

This story is an anchor he'll drag throughout his life,
a sack he can't unpack or drop.
A course between Scylla and Charybdis,
one cliff the weight of fate, his rescue proof
he's marked for something. The power
to do good or else destroy, by accident,
everything he's come to love around him,
moving the story forward, protagonist.

Or, the other cliff, the certainty of randomness,
the knowledge that he doesn't matter, never did.

And if the baby is a girl?
That story never starts.

When a woman walks to the edge of a sea cliff
and doesn't come back, they say
*she's gone to join her selkie lover.*

Which is one way to put it.

If a woman cries seven tears into the ocean,
it's said she'll call a selkie from the waters.
He'll shed his skin where no one sees,
and come by night, searching streets
for sad women.

There are always sad women.

There are women whose salt
calls out to salt, where seaweed
is a wet mat before the waves' pull and tumble.
The body, helpless thing, bats feebly at the tide
until it too is battered.

When they say *sad women*, they mean *unsatisfied.*
They say some women never are.
*Gone to join her lover—*
that selkie might come back.
He might be waiting,
might never have left her.
He might be following her everywhere.

The seals know when there's someone on the cliff top.
Their eyes are wet stones.
In a village with a harbour, there are always sad women.
Every village with a harbour guards a cliff.

TROLL

Naturally I am part troll.
A troll girl from way back.
Although you can't see my teeth.
I sunburn easily and prefer the dark
corners of libraries.
My temperament, I am told,
can be disagreeable.
I like my steak rare
and my fish raw.
When someone tells me to smile,
I bare my fangs. My night vision is excellent.
I have no fear of walking alone.

The advantage to being part troll
is that nobody knows which part.
I wear what I like.
Some evenings I shed my skin, hang out
under bridges, chew rocks.
Some evenings I watch Netflix and chill.
Being fair, I pass for human.
My darker cousins live inside stones.
My family tree, groaning under the weight
of ancestors, would like to drop this branch.
But you can't turn your back on being a troll.
So tell your stories. I won't be petrified.
I worship older gods than you.

One on the back road.
Two on the highway's edge.
One in the berry patch.
One on the bookshelf.
Two making dark calls at night.
Three cruising streets in muscle cars.
One in the alley with a baseball bat.
One in the corner of the brain, waiting until sleep
to come out.

At 50, my body says *fuck it,*
*I'm not following rules anymore.*
One foot on the dock, one foot in a canoe,
a tipping point, two halves of a pill capsule broken open.
This is it: the beginning of the long dash.
My skin sprouts wires, warts, I'm fat
and bony at the same time.
Aphasic, I've discarded conjunctions,
speak only in aphorism, a crone's gnomic utterance.
Knees, long silent, start to talk.
The body's chorus shouts discordantly,
spine a separating zipper.
I am my own uncanny double, zombie,
Frankenstein's creation with dissolving stitches.
Each morning I rise from the dead,
accompanied by creaks and groans.
All day I lurch from point to point,
car with timing belt about to go.
Live fast, die young—too late.
Instead, I'll coddle my corpse-to-be,
prescribed, medicated, moisturized, massaged,
monstrous, and cool with that.

In the '70s, our parents had a yogurt maker and a tortilla press.
They ate dandelions that grew in our lawn
and made their own granola.

In the '70s, we drank
powdered milk and ate carob,
neither of which tasted like our mother claimed they did.
We walked down the street by ourselves
and rang someone's doorbell to say
*can you come out to play?*

In the '70s, our grandparents lived on the corner
and we climbed into our yellow wagon to see them
so often the wheels wore out. My bike
had a bell and a basket, and once I rode around the block
shirtless as a boy.

In the '70s, the TV didn't always broadcast
and we sat in front of coloured bands
waiting for the test pattern to resolve itself.
We turned the laundry stoop into a ship
and the ship into a launch pad.

In the '70s, we moved with our mother
to the edge of town, where there was nothing behind us
but a grid laid out, waiting to be divided.

The future is peevish and elderly.
*You should have started moisturizing your neck,*
*why did you spend that money*
*on coffee?* Hindsight's
a curse, an endless complaint.
You shouldn't have stopped flossing,
should have exercised more.
The past, errant child,
is an endless disappointment
that never makes the grade,
burning all its bridges before it comes to them.
Those second bottles of wine were bad ideas,
as was that second marriage.
Who decided to put birth control pills
down the toilet? Easier to say no
to resistance, earbuds blocking
the anticipated lecture.
No one really wants to see the future,
one wrist slap after another, disaster's starting point
on the horizon in the rearview mirror.

## LOBSTER

We ripped the lobster open
with our bare hands.
When those failed, we used
exquisitely fashioned silver instruments
to rend every scrap of meat
from the hiding places of its shell.
So, yes, I'd like to see your work.
I find myself
hungry, still.

Today we're setting priorities, establishing goals,
getting custody and control of machines.
The Office of Continuous Improvement
improves continuously, and the Visioning Office
revisions.
We've awarded the award
for winning an award, and the library
is closed until further notice.
PIS produce HQPS, as CRCS make CFIS:
faculty are advised to PFO.
Washrooms remain unwashed.
The students—bags of money dressed in skin—
continue to accumulate in gutters and cracks.
Admin is polishing its shell until it sees its face.

# MELT

Ice melts, and the bodies appear.
5,000 years ago, or 50,
they come out just as they went in.
The glacier's tongue retreats, speaking grief.
The past still wears its boots.
The scree's a lost-and-found upended,
accidental specimens strewn across the slope:
a climber on K2, a couple milking cows, passengers
on a final flight, equally preserved.
Without an editor, everything's a clue,
mysterious forests hidden by the trees.

The ice, bad curator, releases exhibits randomly
for us to pounce on. Think
of all we learn, the world a little more
transparent with each degree.
Greedy, we peer at stars without a constellation,
our breath fogging the glass of the display case.
*Why know everything? Because it's there.*

We push back the ice, and viruses come out.
Influenza, anthrax, things we thought we'd put away
come calling. First oceans rise, and now
the mountains too turn traitor.
We thought we had things cased, even corpses
turning into merit badges    *he died*
*doing what he loved!*
Now glaciers return the things we gave them,
debris field showing interruption: notebook,
piece of purple cloth, the snapped branch of a femur
providing useful traction underfoot.
Microbes hold themselves suspended in the ice.
No one thinks they're going to fall.

## CRAWLING

The old man won't admit he's old,
crawls around the lawn because he can't get up,
insisting *I just need more exercise.*
Denial's everywhere now, climate
gone crazy, firestorms, blizzards.
When I was little the first snow
was always on Hallowe'en. Now October opens
with a crisis, hundred-year-old trees snapping,
city collapsing like a crushed umbrella.
The old man has a workaround, invents a story
about how this was what he meant to do.
Old age is a costume, his real self still inside.
His crawling is a choice. A toddler with a blankie,
perversely refusing to eat cake or go to bed,
his brain's short-circuited, memory
a path with shifting markers,
random items surfacing as though from melting ice.
Even crawling, he cranks out rationales,
logic hopscotching from one landmark to another.
Those traffic tickets weren't his fault.
He doesn't need a hearing aid.
He thinks he's in the driver's seat, pugnacious,
refusing to see the drowning beach.

Our little niece can point to north no matter where she is,
and recently started eating paper;
her slightly older sister climbs to the highest point of every playground
but finds writing haiku *quite a challenge.*
The son of friends told his atheist parents that
for their sins Jesus died on the cross
where he was attacked by a shark.
When will the door slam on this world without rules,
where kids head to the Antarctic alone,
self-sufficient, working their way across ice fields
that we can't even see? Small figures, staunch,
charting course decisively, the way a little girl decides one day
that she'll eat paper, that's who she'll be,
the paper eater. Interior lives opaque,
they pinball around the living room, hitting the bumpers
of their own peculiar logics. They don't know yet
the sudden blow from nowhere, or surf's relentless pounding
that grates away the self. Or they do know.
Strange, spiky, they're comets busting through the galaxy,
burning up when they get too close to Earth.

becomes a right of way,
skate-skiers' herringbone
carving the waterway's spine.
Space and time combine
in new perspective: from down here
you can see that the houses of the rich
are crumbling, old cottonwoods
falling into the stream.
Still, we can't get over there,
the river's altered state
allowing only so much movement,
ice tented strangely,
encampment or occupation.
On our side, the river asserts itself,
bubbling up under the bank, dry grass
icicled inside the drip drip drip
of warmer times.
Spring is coming, people say.
Right now, the snow's still falling,
hiding footprints, voices, thin ice,
shielding a sun that's slowly growing.

OPENING

We were goofing around on the road behind the cabin,
taking photos, when the night fell open.
Wolves.
Howling isn't the word for it, there is no word for it.
The way molasses looks when you pour it,
thick, glossy, thinning to a point
before widening out again—that's how it sounds.
Or like running your fingers over a piece of silk, so that
the fabric is perfect but you feel every flaw in your own skin.
We tried recording sound but all we got was noise,
a narrow slice, wood squealing when the axe rips it open.
*What did it sound like?*
Like there was a hole
and we couldn't throw enough into it to fill it up.

## THROWAWAY

The stench was unbelievable,
creature washed up on the beach
an unlikely amalgam of bird, fish, and mammal.
Beaked, finned, and furred, it stank to high heaven.
Seabirds hopped idly through its ribs,
pausing on the spine, the flat skull.
It was very dead, had been for months,
the North Sea flinging it casually onto the rocks,
crabs and gulls industriously carting away its bits.
Now its remains offended us.
We came to the beach for treasure, pink shells,
bits of china, a spoot's sharpened blade.
We didn't come for this, stomach-turning miasma
thrown up on the beach like a bottle slung out of a car window.
Surely it could be hauled away to wherever these things are hauled.
Surely it could be buried. Or burned.
Disgusted, we took photos from all angles,
phones out, holding our breaths.
Structure emerged.
Lines, curves filled the frames, became the frame,
we saw canyon walls, a fallen tree, figures
by Henry Moore, O'Keeffe's shaded sockets.
The rack of bones was now an architecture, balanced,
shifting light inflecting each construction, the aperture
between the ribs a breached boat hull.
I stepped back, uncertain whether what I saw
enhanced the corpse or drained it.
As rotting meat it was specific,
sight and smell carving out the particulars of place.
If it could be these other things?
If art could push out flesh, the way
a wave gave something, clawed it back?
We scoured the beach, cleared the air.
You can look for the creature, but it's gone.

But maybe the tide is already a villanelle,
rolling along with similarity and difference,
not going gentle but still going.
Persistent tide. Seaweed, dead crabs, a shell,
syllables washed up on the beach.
The moon curates, a dip in the night's inkwell.
A villanelle pushes towards inevitability,
unspoken words hanging, hanging
before they break. Recurrence, pleasure
and dread. One inscription overwrites another.
Discipline is key, waves single-minded in their insistence.
Invasion, then recession. We come to the page
knowing what we will find—the unexpected,
a seagull's corpse washed up on the sand.
Inside the verse, discordance. The road's obscured.
Lull, becalmed, the doldrums, water
swirls meaninglessly, mindless erosion.
Then driving force of storm surge, taking us
to the line's end, the shattering. Resonance
sedimentary, cumulative, accretive,
a rolling stone gathering. The tide
picks up, puts down, picks up again,
the image travelling always
to the map's X, that path
the only one we could take.

We parked, locked up, and then killed time,
eyeing the tourists and the deserted island
tempting us across the strait.
The causeway, appearing only at low tide, restricted access
and made us even more intrepid, turning us
(we thought) from sheep to bellwethers.
It was supposed to be low tide.
We kicked rocks, made noise, complained
until we saw the tourists walking on water.
Under the ocean's surface, the causeway shimmered,
as close as it would get to dry land.
Picking our way across, it was hard to tell concrete
from rock, nature nudged by humans.
Once over, I lay in a hole made by Vikings, monks,
or Viking-monks, only sound
the ringing in my ears, until the tourists
chased us out. On the island's far side, we sat
and watched the guillemots make comic landings,
wind flipping them up, surprised umbrellas
suddenly backpedaling, looking offended.
Below us was the invisible shrieking of thousands of birds.
A German tourist strode towards us: *haf you zeen*
*muppins?* Hearing no, she marched away.
The guillemots continued. The causeway weighed on us.
The night before, a tap had dripped, eroding any peace:
this was like that, constant checking of the tide
and fear that it would turn.
At last, making nervous jokes,
we hurried back towards the herd, relieved, anxious
not to be left behind.

## MASS ASCENSION

*Although we have a good understanding of weather and wind*
*patterns and where we might land, we never know exactly*
*where we will touch down.* —TAOS NEWS, OCTOBER 2019

An exhalation overhead, and we look up:
hot air balloons! Like globs of paint squeezed
onto canvas, myriad peas escaping the pod,
their roundness shimmers, tactile, out of reach.
Pre-dawn, they're dumped on the ground, wrapped up
like murder victims, heavy as bodies.
After unbelting, they're massaged into place,
waiting for the fan's hot breath. Soon,
it comes, easing open the envelope's layers,
balloon rising like a soufflé.
Tethered, they billow like bags, roped down like Gulliver.
Then, a signal: flames flash in the silk throat, the burner roars,
the balloon tips up, dragging people, ropes, basket wrestled
        onto the dust.
From earth and fire, they move to air.
Suddenly silent, they ascend, drifting,
radical calm of an astronaut's spacewalk.
From the ground, they're miraculous, lighter than light,
basket the bull's eye of a concentric target.
How must they look to magpies and ravens,
a bird's-eye view seen from below?
A chase car speeds past, one eye to the sky,
and I think of the launch: climbing into the basket,
lighting a spark, the balloon's leap, burner's heat,
upturned faces of my friends as they wave goodbye,
getting smaller and smaller,
nobody knowing where we'll land.

The shape came out of the dark, weird,
hunched, shuffling across the road
as you hit the brakes. A dog?
Maybe, but something wrong.
It kept moving, a straight line,
head down in the headlights.
You pressed the horn and it startled,
sniffing the air, and we realized
it was blind and mostly deaf,
a terrible form more terrible as it moved,
more awful as we realized what this meant.
Head down, it shuffled on.
A car, or bear, or wolf, or someone with a gun
or long, slow suffering in darkness and confusion.
The road gaped under us. We fell in.
Then the shape passed and we drove on,
with the unhappy knowledge that it would get there before us,
but we were heading for the same place.

Chimayó was for crazy people, the kind who think
you can go somewhere on crutches and be healed,
the kind who believe in God.
We went there for the chain-link fences
weighed down with rosaries, the outdoor shrines
deluged by stacks of fabric, candles, other cheap, shiny things.
For the hole in the floor with magic healing dirt (replenished
    twice daily),
presided over by a miraculous crucifix.
Clearly, this was nuts.
My brother was in the hospital for his seventh surgery.
I texted, joking, promising to get him dirt if he promised to eat it.
Wikipedia said that would work.
Coming up from the parking lot, we passed
loose piles of wooden crosses, tossed to the side like discarded
    stage props.
Primitive offerings hung from the fence, god's-eyes
made of twigs and string, crosses built from bent nails and wire,
strips from people's clothes, one step up from animal sacrifice.
A statue showed a white man teaching an "Indian" how to worship.
We moved from the Seven Days Creation Picnic Area
to the Portal of Illumination, traversing geography
outlined by zealots.

Inside, the church was cold but beautiful, flowers frescoed
on the altar, stations of the cross outlined on whitewashed walls.
Candles in two corners offered warmth.
I wandered slowly. It was getting hard to breathe.
I could feel my chest compress, hoped
I wasn't having a conversion experience or allergy attack.
A small door beside the altar: ducking through,
we faced a wall of crutches, walkers, braces,
grouped and stacked to the roof.
The other side was an explosion of photos, big, small,

so many faces, children, old people, hospitals, ball diamonds,
motorcyles, pyjamas, school pictures, floor to ceiling, wall to wall.
I couldn't speak or breathe, couldn't look at other people.
The dirt room was no bigger than a closet; inside,
a blowhard mansplained miracles. I squeezed in.
The room was hot, the walls were close, I wasn't
in my body. My hands were shaking as I knelt, it was hard
to unscrew the jar's lid, important not to spill the magic dirt.
Dust and rocks tipped into my container.
The others fled from this confession.
My desperation filled the room, pushing me outside,
stricken, stuffing the jar into my pocket
before anyone else knew.

"Infinity" and "Science": quotes are from "I Am My Connectome," Sebastian Seung's TED Talk lecture for TED Global 2010, July 2010, at 9:26 and 13:45, respectively. https://www.ted.com/talks/ sebastian_seung_i_am_my_connectome?language=en

"Glia": quote is from "Neurons, Synapses, Action Potentials, and Neurotransmission," by R. Stufflebeam, The Mind Project. https:// mind.ilstu.edu/curriculum/neurons_intro/neurons_intro.html

"Semantic Selectivity": from Ian Sample, "Neuroscientists create 'atlas' showing how words are organised in the brain," in The Guardian, April 27, 2016. https://www.theguardian.com/science/2016/apr/27/ brain-atlas-showing-how-words-are-organised-neuroscience

"Natural Narrative": from Kate Prudchenko, "The Difference Between a Literary and Natural Narrative," penandthepad.com, n.d. https://penandthepad.com/difference-between-literary- natural-narrative-1741.html.

"Supercharged": quote is from "Erich Jarvis, Ph.D., Richard D. Mooney, Ph.D. Neurodegeneration Research Featured in The Scientist," Duke Neurobiology Research News, June 6, 2016. https:// www.neuro.duke.edu/research/research-news/erich-jarvis-phd- richard-d-mooney-phd-neurodegeneration-research-featured

"The Greater Mystery": quoted from "Lighting the Brain: Karl Deisseroth and the optogenetics breakthrough," by John Colapinto, in The New Yorker, May 11, 2015.

Arguments with Agnes Martin: Agnes Martin (1912–2004) was an American painter born in Macklin, Saskatchewan, where she lived until the age of seven. Her best-known works are large, luminous, and sometimes almost colourless canvases marked by lines and grids. Though her work is often described as minimalist, she favoured the idea of abstract expressionism. She lived in New Mexico in the mid-1950s and again from 1968 until her death. In *Agnes Martin: Her Life and Art,* Nancy Princenthal quotes her remark, "I was born in the north of Canada, just like being born in Siberia. The land of no opportunity, that's where I was born." The italicized phrase in "Argument with Agnes Martin (Siberia/Saskatchewan)" is from the Wikipedia description of her work. "Argument with Agnes Martin (Taos)" responds to her statement "I paint with my back to the world."

"Three Marriages: I and the Village" and "The Storm": *I and the Village* is a painting by Marc Chagall, and *The Storm* is a painting by Edvard Munch. Both are viewable at MOMA.

"Throwaway": Spoot is the Orcadian term for a razor shell, a type of shellfish.

"Mass Ascension" is the term for many hot air balloons taking off at the same time, usually at dawn.

"At El Santuario de Chimayó": The sanctuary, one of the most important Catholic pilgrimage sites in North America, is located just outside the town of Chimayó, New Mexico. A miraculous cross was unearthed on this site in 1810, and it is said that dirt from the hole in which the cross was found has healing powers. The statue that the poem refers to is actually of a book-carrying white man enlightening both a Hispanic peasant and a generic Native American. The sanctuary is located on the traditional lands of the Tewa people and sits amidst Nambé, Pojoaque, San Ildefonso, Ohkay Owingeh, Santa Clara, and Tesuque Pueblos.

## ACKNOWLEDGEMENTS

This book was written on Treaty One territory, the traditional
territory of the Anishinaabeg, Cree, Oji-Cree, Dakota, and
Dene Peoples and the homeland of the Métis Nation; and
also on the traditional lands of the people of Taos Pueblo.

Three poems from the Connectomics series were published in CV2
and won the Manitoba Magazine Publishers' Association prize
for poetry. Twelve of the poems were published as an illustrated,
limited-edition chapbook by Jackpine Press (Saskatoon), and 23 were
published in an illustrated version by IRON Press (Cullercoats, UK).
"Winter, and the river" was published in the *Winnipeg Free Press*. A
University of Manitoba Creative Works Grant made possible the
writing of some of these poems. I am grateful for this support.

The Connectomics poems were sparked by a conversation
with a biologist colleague, Mike Shaw. "University
Bulletin" is for my UMFA comrades.

Thanks to the other Plastered Hams, Ariel Gordon and Kerry Ryan,
for their careful reading and comments on the Connectomics poems.
Vanessa Warne, Pam Perkins, and Dana Medoro help me keep my
head above water. Randy Lundy is a scrupulous editor who laughs at
all the right/wrong times. Warren Cariou is my first reader, always.

Alison Calder grew up in Saskatoon. Her poetry has won two Manitoba Book Awards and been a finalist for both the Gerald Lampert Award and the Pat Lowther Award. *Synaptic* is her third collection. In 2000, she moved to Winnipeg, where she teaches Canadian literature and creative writing at the University of Manitoba.

ᐅᗷᑕ

## OSKANA POETRY & POETICS
### BOOK SERIES

Publishing new and established authors, Oskana Poetry
& Poetics offers both contemporary poetry at its best
and probing discussions of poetry's cultural role.

Randy Lundy—*Series Editor*

*Advisory Board*

| | |
|---|---|
| Sherwin Bitsui | Tim Lilburn |
| Robert Bringhurst | Duane Niatum |
| Laurie D. Graham | Gary Snyder |
| Louise Bernice Halfe | Karen Solie |

**PREVIOUS BOOKS IN THE SERIES:**

*Measures of Astonishment: Poets on Poetry,*
presented by the League of Canadian Poets (2016)

*The Long Walk,* by Jan Zwicky (2016)

*Cloud Physics,* by Karen Enns (2017)

*The House of Charlemagne,* by Tim Lilburn (2018)

*Blackbird Song,* by Randy Lundy (2018)

*Forty-One Pages: On Poetry, Language and Wilderness,*
by John Steffler (2019)

*Live Ones,* by Sadie McCarney (2019)

*Field Notes for the Self,* by Randy Lundy (2020)

*Burden,* by Douglas Burnet Smith (2020)

*Red Obsidian,* by Stephan Torre (2021)

*Pitchblende,* by Elise Marcella Godfrey (2021)

*Shifting Baseline Syndrome,* by Aaron Kreuter (2022)

*Synaptic,* by Alison Calder (2022)

CPSIA information can be obtained
at www.ICGtesting.com
Printed in the USA
JSHW031152140422
24926JS00002B/76